Season's Greetings

ISBN 0-7935-9661-0

HAL•LEONARD®
CORPORATION
7777 W. BLUEMOUND RD. P.O. BOX 13819 MILWAUKEE, WI 53213

Visit Hal Leonard Online at
www.halleonard.com

Season's Greetings

CONTENTS

A Caroling We Go

Music and Lyrics by
JOHNNY MARKS

All I Want for Christmas Is You

Words and Music by MARIAH CAREY
and WALTER AFANASIEFF

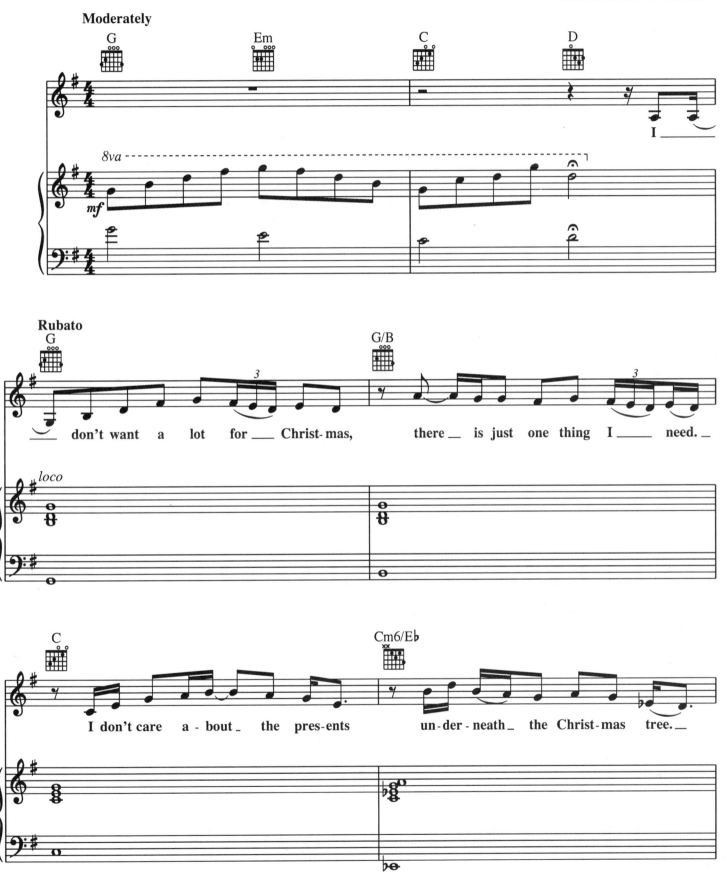

and the sound __ of child - ren's laugh - ter fills __ the air, __

And ev - 'ry - one __ is sing - ing.

I hear those sleigh __ bells ring - ing. San - ta won't you please bring me

what I real - ly need, won't you please bring my ba - by to me. _____ Oh, __

Because It's Christmas
(For All the Children)

Music by BARRY MANILOW
Lyric by BRUCE SUSSMAN and JACK FELDMAN

To-night the stars __ shine__ for the
To-night be-longs__ to __ all the

chil - dren.
chil - dren.

and light the way for dreams³ to
To - night their joy rings__ through the

fly.
air.

To-night³ our love comes wrapped in __
And__ so, we send our ten - der

And _____ so, we send our ten-der bless - ings

to all ___ the chil-dren ___ ev-'ry-where.

To see the smiles _ and hear the laugh - ter; a time _ to

give, a time _ to share be-cause _ it's Christ-mas for now _ and for -

As Long As There's Christmas

FROM WALT DISNEY'S BEAUTY AND THE BEAST - THE ENCHANTED CHRISTMAS

Music by RACHEL PORTMAN
Lyrics by DON BLACK

Blue Christmas

Words and Music by BILLY HAYES
and JAY JOHNSON

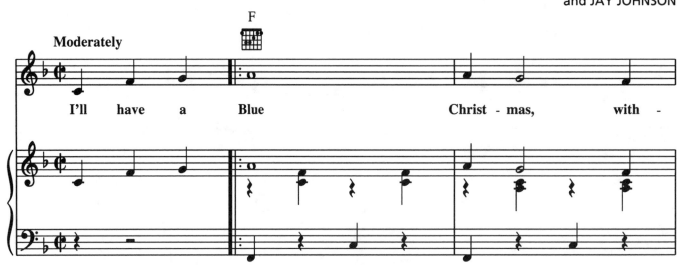

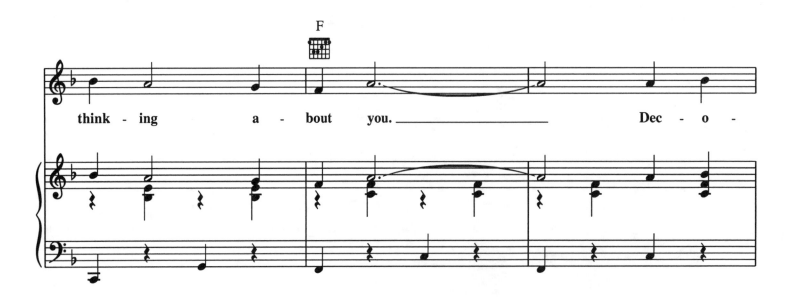

Brazilian Sleigh Bells

By PERCY FAITH

The Chipmunk Song

Words and Music by
ROSS BAGDASARIAN

Christmas Is

Lyrics by SPENCE MAXWELL
Music by PERCY FAITH

Feliz Navidad

Music and Lyrics by
JOSE FELICIANO

CHRISTMAS IS A HOMEMADE HOLIDAY

By ANNIE DINERMAN
and NED GINSBURG

The Christmas Song
(Chestnuts Roasting on an Open Fire)

Music and Lyric by MEL TORME
and ROBERT WELLS

Sentimentally

Chest - nuts roast-ing on an op - en fire, Jack Frost nip - ping at your nose,

Yule - tide car - ols be - ing sung by a choir And folks dressed up like Es - ki - mos. Ev - 'ry - bo - dy

knows a tur - key and some mis - tle - toe___ Help to make the seas - on bright.

The Christmas Waltz

Words by SAMMY CAHN
Music by JULE STYNE

Moderately, with expression

When the world falls in love, Ev'ry song you hear_____ seems to say:_____

"Mer - ry Christ - mas,_____ May your New Year dreams come true."_____

And this song of mine,_____ in three - quar - ter time,_____ Wish - es you and yours_____

the same thing too._____

Deck the Hall

Traditional Welsh Carol

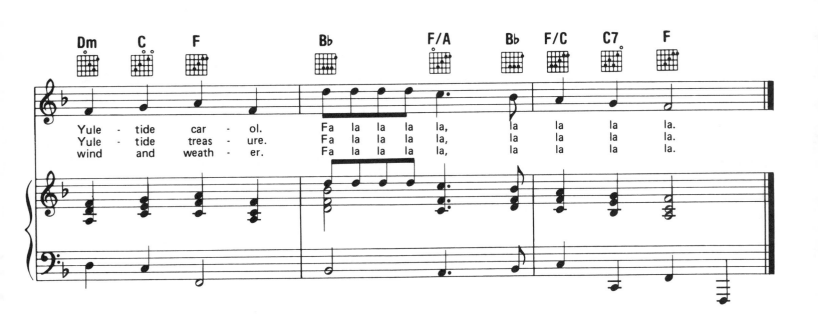

The First Chanukah Night

FROM *YOURS, ANNE*

Words and Music by ENID FUTTERMAN
and MICHAEL COHEN

On the first Cha-nu-kah night we light one Cha-nu-kah

light in mem-'ry of the mir-a-cle of the first Cha-nu-kah night. On the

sec-ond Cha-nu-kah night we light two Cha-nu-kah lights in

mem-'ry of the mir-a-cle of the sec-ond Cha-nu-kah night.

On the

mp

FROSTY THE SNOW MAN

Words and Music by STEVE NELSON
and JACK ROLLINS

Moderato

1. FROS - TY, THE SNOW MAN was a jol - ly hap - py soul,___ With a
2. FROS - TY, THE SNOW MAN knew the sun was hot that day,___ So he

corn cob pipe and a but - ton nose___ and two eyes made out of coal.
said "Let's run and we'll have some fun___ now be - fore I melt a - way."

CHRISTMAS IS A-COMIN'
(MAY GOD BLESS YOU)

Words and Music by
FRANK LUTHER

61

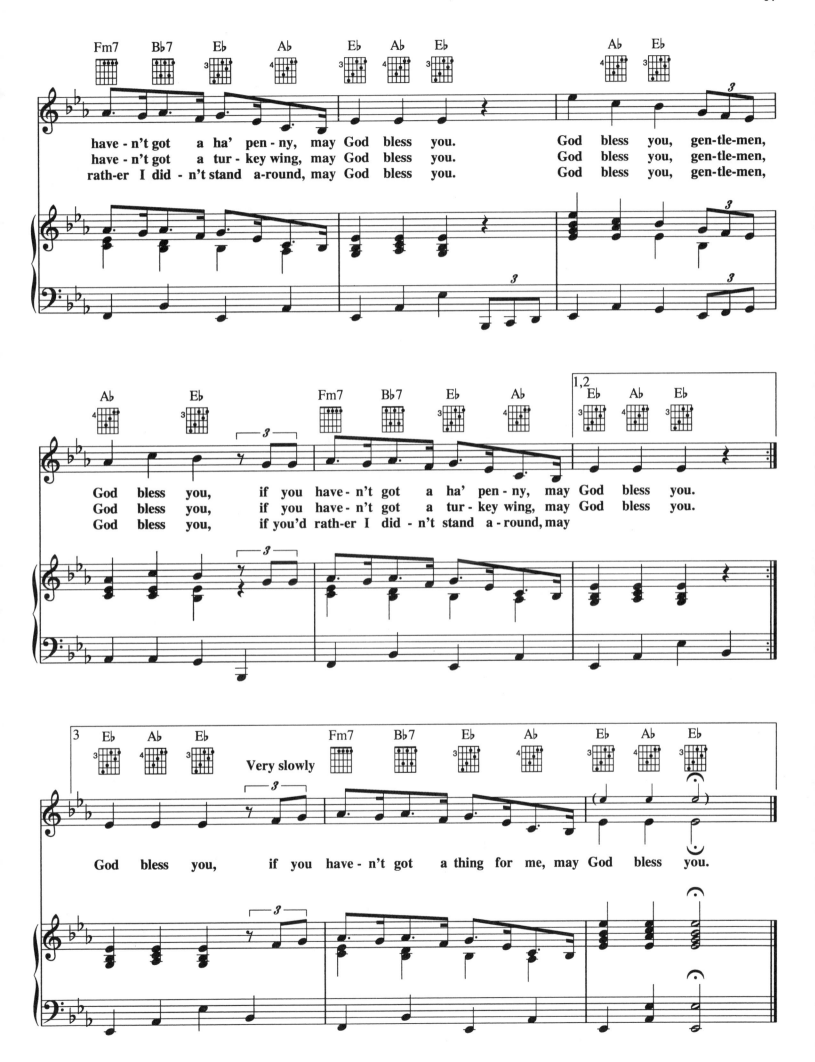

The Gift

Words and Music by TOM DOUGLAS
and JIM BRICKMAN

Female: Hoo. _____

Win - ter snow is fall - ing ___ down, chil - dren laugh - ing all a - round,

lights are turn - ing on, _____ like a fair - y tale ___ come true. ___

GESÙ BAMBINO

Text by FREDERICK H. MARTENS
Music by PIETRO YON

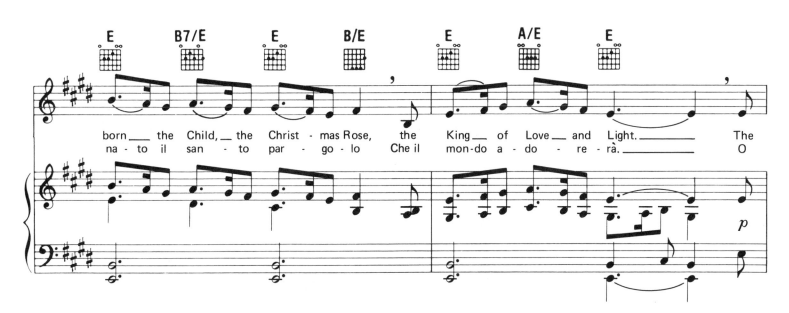

GOD REST YE MERRY, GENTLEMEN

Moderately

19th Century English Carol

Grandma Got Run Over by a Reindeer

Words and Music by
RANDY BROOKS

You can say there's no such thing as San-ta, but as for me and Grand-pa, we be-

lieve. _____

Additional Lyrics

Verse 2:
Now we're all so proud of Grandpa,
He's been taking this so well.
See him in there watching football,
Drinking beer and playing cards with Cousin Mel.
It's not Christmas without Grandma.
All the family's dressed in black,
And we just can't help but wonder:
Should we open up her gifts or send them back?
Chorus

Verse 3:
Now the goose is on the table,
And the pudding made of fig,
And the blue and silver candles,
That would just have matched the hair in Grandma's wig.
I've warned all my friends and neighbors,
Better watch out for yourselves.
They should never give a license
To a man who drives a sleigh and plays with elves.
Chorus

GRANDMA'S KILLER FRUITCAKE

Words and Music by ELMO SHROPSHIRE
and RITA ABRAMS

The Greatest Gift of All

Words and Music by
JOHN JARVIS

Dawn is slow - ly break - ing,—
our friends have all___ gone home.
You and I are
wait - ing_ for San - ta Claus to come.

HAPPY HOLIDAY

FROM THE MOTION PICTURE IRVING BERLIN'S HOLIDAY INN

Words and Music by
IRVING BERLIN

HAPPY CHRISTMAS, LITTLE FRIEND

Lyrics by OSCAR HAMMERSTEIN II
Music by RICHARD RODGERS

The soft morn-ing light of a pale win-ter sun is trac-ing the trees on the snow. Leap up lit-tle friend and fly down the stairs for Christ-mas is wait-ing be-low. There's a

Happy Xmas
(War Is Over)

Words and Music by JOHN LENNON
and YOKO ONO

Hark! The Herald Angels Sing

Words by CHARLES WESLEY
Music by FELIX MENDELSSOHN-BARTHOLDY

Home
(When Shadows Fall)

Words and Music by GEOFF CLARKSON,
HARRY CLARKSON and PETER VAN STEEDEN

I Heard the Bells on Christmas Day

Words by HENRY WADSWORTH LONGFELLOW
Music by JOHN BAPTISTE CALKIN

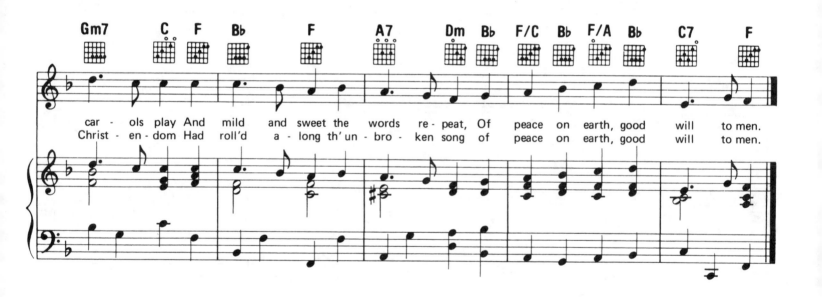

3. And in despair I bow'd my head:
   "There is no peace on earth," I said,
   "For hate is strong, and mocks the song
   Of peace on earth, good will to men."

4. Then pealed the bells more loud and deep:
   "God is not dead, nor doth He sleep;
   The wrong shall fail, the right prevail,
   With peace on earth, good will to men."

5. Till, ringing, singing on its way,
   The world revolved from night to day,
   A voice, a chime, a chant sublime,
   Of peace on earth, good will to men!

I'll Be Home for Christmas

Words and Music by KIM GANNON
and WALTER KENT

Moderately slow

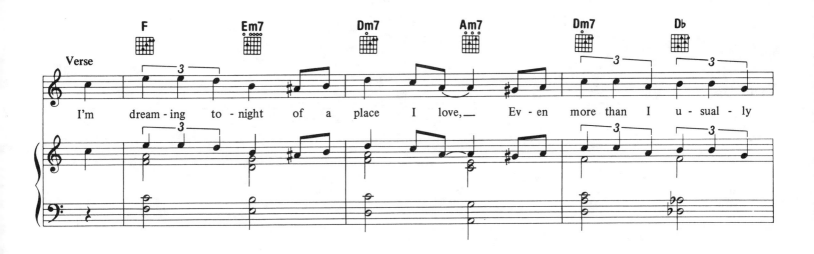

I'm dream-ing to-night of a place I love,___ Ev-en more than I u-sual-ly

do.___ And al-though I know it's a long road back,___ I prom-ise

I Saw Mommy Kissing Santa Claus

Words and Music by
TOMMIE CONNOR

Moderately slow

I saw Mom-my kiss-ing San - ta Claus, un-der-neath the mis-tle-toe last night._____ She did-n't see me creep down the stairs to have a peep, she thought that I was tucked up in my bed-room fast a-

I Still Believe in Santa Claus

Words and Music by MAURICE STARR
and AL LANCELLOTTI

It Must Have Been the Mistletoe
(Our First Christmas)

By JUSTIN WILDE
and DOUG KONECKY

IT'S CHRISTMAS IN NEW YORK

Words and Music by
BILLY BUTT

Jingle-Bell Rock

Words and Music by JOE BEAL
and JIM BOOTHE

Jingle Bells

Words and Music by
J. PIERPONT

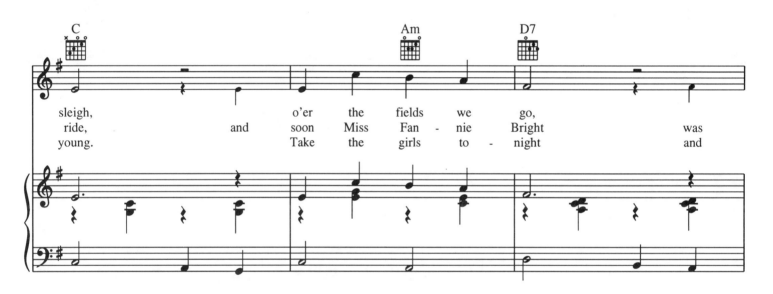

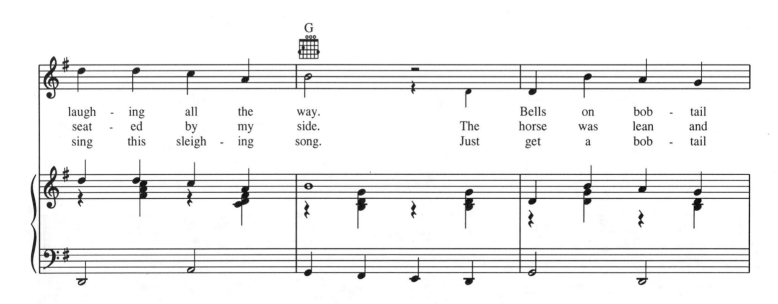

Last Christmas

Words and Music by
GEORGE MICHAEL

Spoken: Happy Christmas

Ah, _____ oo, woh, _____

JOY TO THE WORLD

Words by ISAAC WATTS
Music by GEORGE F. HANDEL

With spirit

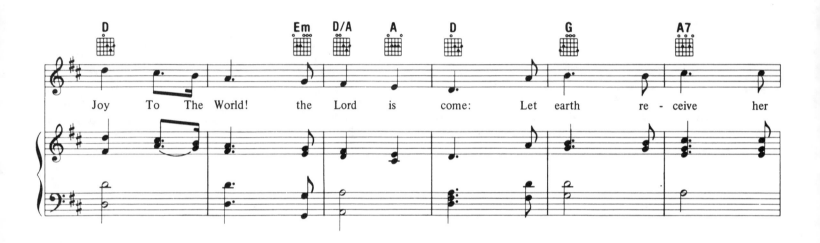

Joy To The World! the Lord is come: Let earth re - ceive her

King; Let ev - ery heart pre - pare Him room, And heaven and na - ture

LET IT SNOW! LET IT SNOW! LET IT SNOW!

Words by SAMMY CAHN
Music by JULE STYNE

Most of All I Wish You Were Here

Music and Lyrics by
DENISE OSSO

Moderately slow

Your gift ar-rived the first day it snowed. I laid it un-der the tree.

I lit a fire, think-ing a-bout how much you've giv-en me. I

thought a-bout how luck-y we are though we're so far a-part.

O LITTLE TOWN OF BETHLEHEM

Words by PHILLIPS BROOKS
Music by LEWIS H. REDNER

O Christmas Tree

Traditional German Carol

Christ - mas tree! O Christ - mas tree, you stand in ver - dant beau - ty! O O
Christ - mas tree! O Christ - mas tree, much plea - sure doth thou bring me! O O
Christ - mas tree! O Christ - mas tree, thy can - dles shine out bright - ly! O O

Christ - mas tree, O Christ - mas tree, you stand in ver - dant beau - ty! Your
Christ - mas tree, O Christ - mas tree, much plea - sure doth thou bring me! For
Christ - mas tree, O Christ - mas tree, thy can - dles shine out bright - ly! Each

O HOLY NIGHT

French Words by PLACIDE CAPPEAU
English Words by D.S. DWIGHT
Music by ADOLPHE ADAM

Santa, Bring My Baby Back
(To Me)

Words and Music by CLAUDE DeMETRUIS
and AARON SCHROEDER

Bright rock

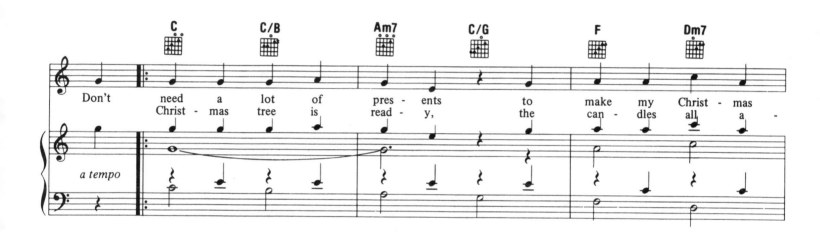

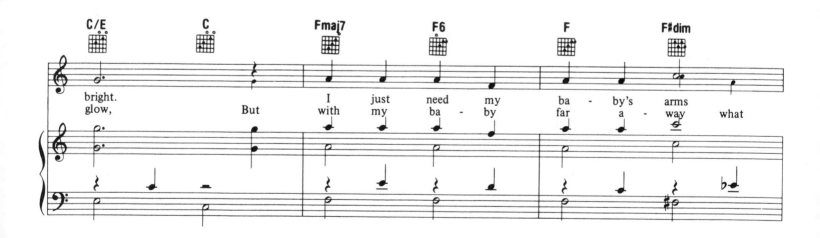

Please Come Home for Christmas

Words and Music by CHARLES BROWN
and GENE REDD

year ____ to be ____ with the one you love. ____

So won't you tell ___ me ___ you'll ___ nev - er - more _
(Instrumental)

___ roam. ____ Christ - mas and New Year ____

will ___ find you home. ____ *(Instrumental ends)* Ooo There'll be no more

Rudolph the Red-Nosed Reindeer

Music and Lyrics by
JOHNNY MARKS

Silent Night

Words by JOSEPH MOHR
Music by FRANZ GRÜBER

SNOWFALL

Lyrics by RUTH THORNHILL
Music by CLAUDE THORNHILL

Silver Bells
FROM THE PARAMOUNT PICTURE THE LEMON DROP KID

Words and Music by JAY LIVINGSTON
and RAY EVANS

Christ-mas makes you feel e-mo-tion-al. It may bring par-ties or thoughts de-vo-tion-al. What-ev-er hap-pens or what may be, Here is what Christ-mas time means to

We Wish You a Merry Christmas

Traditional English Folksong

Brightly

We

wish you a Mer-ry Christ-mas, We wish you a Mer-ry Christ-mas, We

wish you a Mer-ry Christ-mas, and a hap-py New Year. Good

WHAT MADE THE BABY CRY?

Words and Music by
WILLIAM J. GOLAY

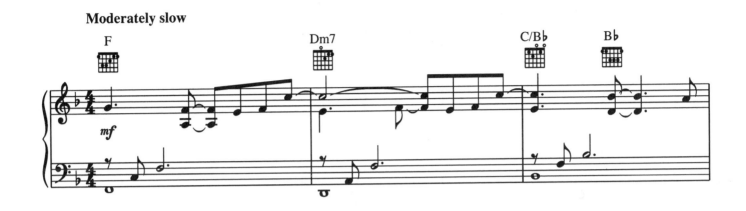

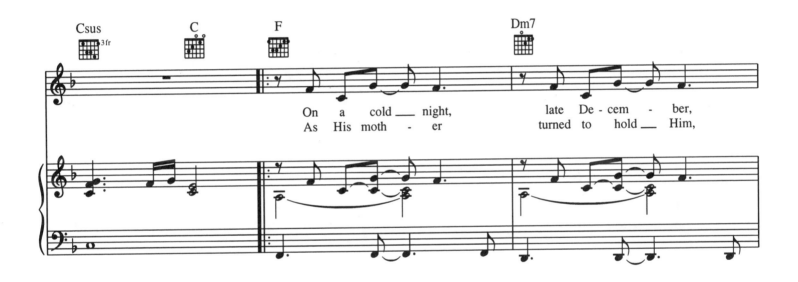

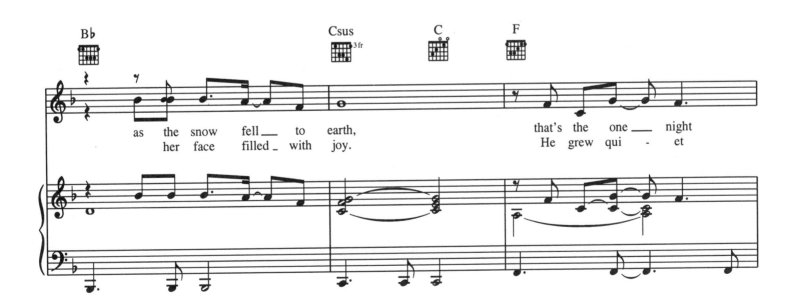

WONDERFUL CHRISTMASTIME

Words and Music by
McCARTNEY